HOW TO AVOID PROBATE

. . . Like the Plague

David Goodhart

WRITEWAY PUBLISHING
Raleigh, North Carolina
www.writewaypublishing.com

How to Avoid Probate . . . Like the Plague

DISCLAIMER:

This book is not intended as a substitute or replacement for individualized advice from an attorney for your own particular situation. The purchase or reading of this book does not create any kind of professional relationship between the author or the publisher and the reader. Laws and processes vary from state to state, and the opportunities mentioned in this book may not be available in your state or may not suit your purposes. Consult a qualified attorney in your state for specific legal advice.

ISBN 978-1-956543-75-9
Printed in the United States of America
Cover by 100Covers

WRITEWAY PUBLISHING
Raleigh, North Carolina
www.writewaypublishing.com

CONTENTS

Introduction

The "Black Death," oftentimes referred to colloquially as the Plague, was a devastating pandemic that swept through Europe and Asia in the mid-1300s, resulting in an estimated 25 to 75 million deaths. It is considered one of the deadliest pandemics in human history.

Probate is a very much misunderstood process that sooner or later, one way or another, will unnecessarily affect most of us. **It is the legal process of administering the disposition of the estate of a deceased person, with or without a Will.**

You might think this disposition will have a quick, simple, and obvious outcome, but that's not true. Not by a long shot. **I liken it to contracting the plague, something to be avoided at all costs.**

To be sure, it requires an attorney to file for probate with the appropriate probate court and usually entails more than one court hearing. And that's just the start. The probate process regularly delivers headaches and often creates heartaches. It takes time, and it costs money—your heirs' money, in fact.

While everything I write in this book is Texas-specific, the truth of the matter is that these concepts—why we should avoid probate and how to do it—are applicable to everyone across all 50 states, though the measures taken to accomplish this vary somewhat across the states.

It is quite safe to say it would be very wise to avoid probate. But is that even possible? And, if it is possible, how do we make that happen?

The good news is that there are simple measures that can resolve most probate-related issues. The harder part is knowing what those measures are. **Let me be absolutely clear: everybody in the United States should be attempting to avoid probate. And that's the bottom line.**

That's what this book is about: **how to avoid probate.**

My own law practice is singularly designed to keep people out of probate. And, while I joke about avoiding probate like avoiding the plague, the repercussions of having to go to probate can truly be devastating to families. Thankfully, avoiding probate nowadays is relatively simple with a little proactive preparation.

First, you have to know the **best question** to ask from the start (revealed in an upcoming chapter) and then determine what steps you need to take in your situation to protect your family from probate.

If you are not a resident of Texas, you can ask the same best question and follow the solutions for your state.

This book is designed to help you know what to ask and offers specific solutions in the State of Texas. For non-Texans, use the guidance in this book as part of your question process for determining your own plan to avoid probate.

Since you now know you can avoid probate for your estate, one of my favorite questions to ask clients is "why on earth would you voluntarily subject yourself or your family to something that is as costly, time-consuming, and painful as probate when you don't have to?"

Follow the simple measures outlined in this guide and protect your estate for your family after you are gone.

1

Common Estate Myths (That Keep Families Trapped)

An overwhelming majority of Americans have a relatively simple estate, perhaps only owning a home and a bank account to pass along to their heirs. This is all the more reason to keep things clean and simple and provide a way for the heirs to receive the most benefit from the estate left to them.

There's absolutely no need to go to probate to make sure that the house and those bank accounts make it to your loved ones. But steps have to be taken while you are alive to ensure probate can be avoided, because otherwise, be assured, probate will be involved.

People say:

> *"I want to get a Will because I want to tell people what happens to my stuff after I die."*

Well, that's great and at least they are planning.

But if all you are relying on is a Will, you are in trouble!!! Sure, if you write in your Will, "I leave all my stuff to my wonderful spouse," then, yes, your spouse is going to get all your stuff. Eventually.

Yes, the spouse will receive your assets, but he or she will not get one single dime until the Will is probated. The spouse does not "automatically" receive everything as many people assume. The Will must go through the entire probate process at the probate court before the spouse can legally gain access to your assets.

Let's start by clearing the air right now—because the probate system thrives on these myths.

If any of these sound familiar, you're not alone:

- "We have a Will, so we won't need probate."
- "My spouse will automatically inherit everything."
- "If I'm named executor, I can just take care of it."
- "My lawyer already set this up—we're good."
- "Probate only happens if you don't have a Will."
- "I don't have that much—probate won't apply to me."

- "We'll figure it out when the time comes."
- "My joint bank accounts already go to my spouse, right?"
- "Wills are what responsible people do."

Every single one of those statements is either completely false or dangerously misleading. I bet you thought the last point was good—doing a reasonable thing—but, no, it is not, if you stop there.

A Story to Start Us Off

Not long ago, a woman walked into my office, clearly upset. Her father had passed away a few months earlier, and she was stuck. He had told her everything was taken care of—said he had a Will, that everything would be smooth. But now? She was six months in, out thousands of dollars, and still couldn't access a single account. She looked at me and said, "I feel like I'm being punished for trusting him."

That stuck with me.

Because he tried to do a responsible thing.

He didn't mean to leave a mess.

He just didn't know what he didn't know.

And neither did she.

The Psychology of "Doing the Responsible Thing"

Here's the part that gets me.

Most people walk into a lawyer's office and say something like, *"I want to do the responsible thing to take care of my family after my death."*

And the lawyer nods and prepares a Will for them.

They walk out with a folder under their arm feeling like they did something good.

Like they've protected their family.

Like they checked the grown-up box.

And what do they do with that folder?

They put it in a drawer. Or a filing cabinet. Or tuck it away somewhere and forget about it. They don't touch it for their remaining years.

But what they don't realize is that they have created a tremendous problem for their family. They literally locked the problem in a drawer.

That Will doesn't keep their family out of the probate court. ***It sends them straight to the probate court.***

So what they thought was "responsible" was really just what the industry conditioned them to believe.

It's not your fault if that's what you thought too. The industry is replete with dodgy probate lawyers who need you to go to probate in order to collect thousands of dollars in fees. That's how they make their living.

But now that you know better after reading this book, you've got a chance to do better for your family.

Here's the deal. The only way for a Will to have any legal force or effect is taking it through the entire probate process. And, to be clear, that means the probate court. I like to compare this to Dr. Frankenstein and his monster. You remember that scene where the lightning bolt gives the monster life? Same thing with a Will. *Until the probate court zaps the Will to life, it's worthless paper.*

You wouldn't be alone if you didn't know that.

Let's just say, then, that probate is the price of not planning correctly. And more often than not, it's a totally unnecessary price.

There are better, faster, and cleaner ways to pass your assets to your loved ones than through a Will.

2

How This Approach Is Different

Most estate planning starts and ends with a Will. It's what people ask for. It's what most lawyers unfortunately provide. I actually wrote a book about Wills. It's called *Bad Things Happen When You Die Without a Will.* Because they do, especially if you have no other estate measures in place.

My goal, however, is to go one step further and leave assets to your loved ones and **keep them out of probate at the same time. Period.**

You don't want your family in a courtroom.

You don't want them paying a lawyer after you're gone.

You don't want them wasting months fighting over paperwork or waiting for a judge to sign off on something that needs to be done or accessed.

You don't want any of those things for your family. I don't want those things for your family either.

You want your family to inherit cleanly, quickly, and privately what you've built in your lifetime and then left for them. I want the same for you and them.

And that means thinking differently.

It means you asking a better question than "do you do Wills?" from the start. When you are planning your estate disposition, here's the **best question** to ask that I promised you in the Introduction of this book: ***How do we avoid probate altogether?***

That's the starting point, the shift in handling the disposition of your estate.

There are big-ticket decisions to deal with now in life and in designating your estate plans—buying property, property ownership, titling accounts, and planning for the future—and these decisions deserve more than guesswork or depending on some generic off-the-rack legal form with no professional advice.

I can't tell you how many people come to me with problems that could have been solved years earlier if they'd just gotten proper direction.

Avoiding probate starts with being willing to seek professional advice from someone who actually knows how to keep you out of probate. You don't know what you don't know! That's why starting with the **best question** is so important.

This is not about spending more money now. It's about spending wisely—and early—so your loved ones don't have to spend time and a lot more money later.

Helping people completely avoid probate has become my mission in life. And I've set a goal to help 10,000 families avoid being casualties of probate. I'm well on my way to making that happen.

For now, let's remove your family from the future casualties of probate list.

3

Why Do People End Up in Probate?

Most heirs end up in probate because of the decedent's inaction while they were alive: they didn't do any estate planning or depended on a basic Will to "take care" of everything in their estate for their family.

Here's the data:

According to a 2023 Caring.com survey, only **32 percent of Americans have a Will or any form of estate planning document** in place. And here's the problem with that—of those who have made the effort to create a Will, nearly all of them think they're covered "for life" and never look at it again. They don't realize that to give the Will any legal effect, it has to be submitted to the probate court and be probated.

So, how about the rest of the people—those that don't even have a Will? Same problem: but they are going to the probate court twice—once to determine who the decedent's heirs at law are and then once more to probate the estate.

Again, not knowing this is not your fault. Americans have been brainwashed into thinking that they need a Will. People often call me and say, "David, do you do Wills?" And I'll always tell them something like, "Of course I do Wills, but that's not the end goal. The end goal is not to need a Will." That stumps them.

Not only is a Will not the best solution, I argue it's often the problem.

The overwhelming majority of Americans believe that if they have a Will, they're set. They think having the Will automatically handles everything when they die. But here's the reality of that. That Will sitting in a desk drawer or wherever it is tucked away—well, it has no legal power on its own. As I noted earlier, a Will is worthless paper until it's been submitted to the probate court and formally blessed by the probate judge.

By relying on just a Will, you think you are doing the right thing, but actually you have guaranteed your family a trip to the probate court.

I sometimes tell clients that a Will isn't really a shield—it's more like a shovel. It digs the family deeper into the probate process.

And that process? It's slow. It's expensive. It's public. And, by Texas law, it requires a lawyer.

People don't realize that by choosing to distribute their estate via a Will, they are guaranteeing probate. They are opting into a system that requires them—or more accurately, their loved ones—to navigate months of court paperwork, hearings, and fees.

Let me tell you about the $300 Will that cost $9,000.

A few years ago, I had a guy come in after his mother died. She'd done what she thought was the right thing. She got a Will from a lawyer. He worked out of a strip center. Same guy did traffic tickets and divorces. Charged her 300 bucks. Whole thing was two pages.

"We're good," the son said, holding it up like it was a prize.

I asked, "Did she file a Transfer on Death Deed on the house?"

Blank stare.

"Any beneficiary designations on her bank accounts?"

Nothing.

That $300 Will? It cost him over $9,000 in legal fees once probate was all said and done, and it took eight months to settle.

And that's with no drama. No fighting. No disputes. Just the pure, raw drag of probate.

The History of the Will Trap

Back in the 1800s, probate was a necessary evil. There were no computers. No banks with easy-to-access records. If someone died, the only way to verify who got what was through a judge.

So the Will became the gold standard. The responsible thing. The grown-up document.

And the legal industry?

We wrapped our arms around it.

By the early 1900s, we had built an entire system around the Will. Probate courts. Filing fees. Executor appointments. Hearings. Statutes. Rules. Whole law firms existed just to move paper from one office to another—all under the banner of "doing it the right way."

Now fast forward to today.

We've got technology. Online deeds. Banking automation. Title companies that process ownership overnight.

But what do most people still walk out of the lawyer's office with?

A Will.

And a false sense of security.

Why?

Because the system never evolved. And, the fact that probate lawyers make a lot of money going to probate.

So here we are—150 years later—still telling families to trust a piece of paper that guarantees court involvement after they're gone.

4

The Top 5 Mistakes That Guarantee Probate

Let me break this down real clear.

You want to know why people end up in probate?

These five mistakes show up in almost every estate I've ever had to clean up:

Mistake #1: Titling assets in your own name only.

If the deed to the house says "John Smith" and John dies, that property's going to probate. Every time.

Mistake #2: Forgetting to add POD or TOD designations.

Bank accounts. Brokerage accounts. The house. If there's no "Payable on Death" (POD) feature on your bank accounts or "Transfer on Death" (TOD) filed for your house, they're going to probate by default. Yes, I will explain more about these designations in an upcoming chapter in this book.

Mistake #3: Outdated or missing beneficiary designations.

I've seen life insurance policies that still name an ex-spouse—or no one at all. That means delay, confusion, and court intervention.

Mistake #4: Thinking a Will overrides everything else.

If your TOD says one thing and your Will says another, the TOD wins. Every time. But people think the Will is the master key—it's not.

Mistake #5: Doing a Will and never reviewing it again.

Did you get married? Have kids? Buy property? Divorce? Change banks? Remarry? Have more children? You'd better believe your old Will didn't update itself.

Any of these are guaranteed to create issues in estate distribution if they have not been addressed prior to your death. These are fixable mistakes. But only if you create an estate plan before it's too late.

5

The Wild Wonderful World of Probate

Let me take you inside what I call *The Wild Wonderful World of Probate.* And just so we're clear—that's me being sarcastic.

It's not really wonderful, but it really is wild. It's also a slow, expensive, lawyer-designed maze. A system *built by lawyers, for lawyers,* dressed up in official-sounding paperwork and court processes that most families never see coming—until it's too late to do anything about it.

And once you're in probate? You're not getting out without time, money, and legal firepower.

You see, in the probate world, the Will has to be submitted to the probate court by a lawyer. Not you. (Remember, the Will does not come into play while you are alive.) Not by a member or members of your family, unless one is a lawyer.

Probate lawyers were very clever and created a system where you have to hire a lawyer to go through the entire probate system. And that's expensive.

A lawyer has to submit the Will to the probate court, file some other documents along the way, and then, maybe five or six months later, because the docket stays full, there'll be a hearing scheduled.

Now comes the real problems. I talked about these things in my book *Bad Things Happen When You Die Without a Will.*

Once the estate is opened, it's public. That means everyone—good or bad—gets a shot at your family's money. Creditors. Distant relatives. Strangers. Whoever. Even fictitious claims against an estate happen more than you might think. At some point, it all has to be vetted.

And all that chaos can be avoided by easy actions you can take now, while you are still alive. Let's look at this further.

To start with, if an asset is titled in your own name, it is characterized as a **probate asset.** This gives the court jurisdiction over that asset, because the probate court has jurisdiction over probate assets. Once the Will is submitted to the probate court and five or six months have passed, the court will ultimately have a hearing and bless your Will. At that hearing, an executor will be appointed, usually the one recommended in your Will, to handle the disposition of your probate assets.

Note that the person you recommended in your Will—even if you named your spouse or an adult child—will not automatically become your executor. The judge will vet that person to make sure they qualify under the laws of the state to act as executor of your Will.

If everything works out according to plan, great. That executor will be appointed to carry out the duties of handling your estate, and the judge will issue a certificate to the executor called Letters Testamentary. This allows the executor to distribute your assets according to the specific wishes identified in your Will.

I liken Letters Testamentary to something from the movie *Willy Wonka & the Chocolate Factory.* Remember the golden ticket in the Wonka bar?

That's what the Letters Testamentary are—golden tickets. Once the executor has that, the executor is golden. It's as if they've stepped into the shoes of the decedent. They can do whatever the decedent could've done. Open a bank account. Close one. Buy property. Sell property. Borrow money. You name it.

But of course, the executor's also wearing a fiduciary hat. They've got to follow the instructions in the Will.

What happens if there is no Will? Instead of Letters Testamentary, the court issues Letters of Administration. Instead of an executor, you've got a court appointed administrator for your estate. Probably a stranger. Once the administrator has those Letters of Administration, they're golden. Now they can do whatever the decedent could've done, but they and the court, not you, decide what to do with your assets, because you did not make a Will or leave any appropriate instructions for the disposing of your estate. **And your family will have to pay for this service.**

Once an executor or administrator is appointed—each one does the same thing—he or she make decisions about and distributes the probate assets of that particular estate. The executor, of course, by following the instructions in your Will; the administrator by applying the laws of intestacy in distributing assets because you left no instructions as there was no Will.

So, what happens if the person named in the Will—say, your son—is the only one who could realistically serve as executor, but, unfortunately, he went through a rough patch, and he's got a felony on his record? Remember that the judge has to vet the person who will be acting as executor of your Will, and there are laws that guide the judge's decision to approve the executor.

One such requirement is that the executor cannot have a felony conviction. There's actually an oath the executor must take—it's a true oath. It begins something like: I, David Goodhart, never having been convicted of a felony or a crime of moral turpitude. . . " and continues on from there. In other words, the prospective executor has to swear an oath, and swearing falsely can really cause trouble!

That means, in this case of the son with a felony conviction, the court's going to say, "No, the son can't be the executor." Then the court will need to **hire an attorney** to handle this estate instead. It gets worse. Who pays that attorney? The heirs.

That's right. That's exactly correct. That could happen.

Let's just for a minute go one step further. Suppose you die without a Will (called dying intestate) and leave no direct heirs. In such cases, the State of Texas steps in and takes your assets. Yes, they do. It's called "escheating," and it's the law. It's 100 percent legal.

This is just part of the whole craziness of probate. You can see why I call it the wild wonderful world of probate—because it is. I mean, who on Earth would want to be a part of that?

Here's what most people dealing with an estate don't realize—they're part of a multi-billion-dollar system that thrives on probate.

In Texas according to probatecourtbond.com, the estate-planning world—probate lawyers, courts, clerks—is now a **$6 billion annual industry,** which makes up a large part of a legal services complex. Probate lawyers have become independently wealthy hoping and praying all you are relying on is a Will.

What that means for families like you and yours is staggering—**probate can eat up a substantial chunk of your estate**, and those court delays, cleverly orchestrated by the lawyers involved, including yours, can stretch a year or more. So an estate valued at $350,000 could lose approximately *$3,500 to thousands more* in fees alone—because someone's got to file all those documents and show up to all of those hearings.

Let me be absolutely blunt—it's no accident this system makes you think a Will is all you need.

I once asked a probate lawyer why they always offer a Will first. He shrugged and said, "It gets them in the door." I replied, "What?"

You see, the Will is the bait—you think you're doing right by your family.

The probate work is the payoff.

Courts, clerks, appraisers, attorneys—are waiting on the back end. Your family pays for that system.

6

Getting Probate Started

So, now that we have discussed estate executors and administrators, let's go a bit further into the world of probate.

Before the probate court ever sees a Will, someone has to file an application, letting the world know that an estate has been opened.

And once that happens, buckle up.

Anyone who thinks they have a claim against the estate can show up. Sometimes it's just the family's lawyer. But not always. There could be multiple lawyers, creditors, distant relatives, or others, because now they've been invited to the table.

Dealing with all this can get expensive. Fast.

Eventually—five or six months later—the court will schedule a hearing. Everybody who wants to appear can appear. Heirs don't always have to come to court. But usually the applicant shows up. That's often the surviving spouse or the child who initiated the probate.

And this is all assuming that everything's gone right so far. We're also assuming the Will is not being contested. That nobody's claiming they're an heir when others think they're not. That there's no drama.

That no drama situation does not always happen, but that's a whole other legal, and expensive, thing.

Dependent Administration or Independent Administration

In Texas, we have two different kinds of probate. One is called a dependent administration and the other is called an independent administration.

Let's continue the discussion of everything going smoothly. There's a hearing. The judge dusts off the Will—sticks the electrodes into it, so to speak—and like I said before, gives it life. Assuming it's a valid Texas Will, of course.

But here's the sad news: even at this point, it doesn't get easier. It's time to determine if the Will is to be administered under dependent administration or independent administration.

In a **dependent administration,** the executor or administrator has to ask the court for permission every single time they want to do something.

Sharpen an estate pencil (okay, a small exaggeration). Sell property. Make a distribution. Open a bank account. Close a bank account. Every single action requires filing a motion with the court, giving all of the related parties a chance to object, and waiting for the court to give a ruling on the requested action. It can be a circus.

Dependent administration is slow. It's expensive. There are hundreds of probates being supervised in every county at any given time. Hundreds. That's how it works.

And it drags grieving families through a legal maze that could've easily been avoided with the second kind of administration. So, what's the other option?

Independent administration, on the other hand, is where, once appointed, the executor is off and running. He or she doesn't have to report back to the court for anything. Not until everything's done and the estate is closed. At that point, the executor files a final document, indicating they have done everything they were supposed to do. And that's it. The executor is out.

You're probably thinking, "Well, hold on. I want *that* one. I want the independent version. How do I get that?"

Good question.

Interestingly—and this will blow your mind—you just have to ask for it. Who asks? You do when you are preparing your Will. And how do you ask for this? In the body of the Will.

You literally include an instruction in your Will that you want your executor to serve independently. That's all you have to do: ask for that independence with a simple instruction in your Will.

What happens if you don't include that instruction? Your estate falls under dependent administration. Automatically.

Most people don't know this. They don't know they have to ask for independent administration in their Will. Their lawyer should know that, but what advantage is it to the lawyer to ensure that the estate will be processed under independent administration? Did I just say that some lawyers might "accidentally forget" to make sure the Will includes a request for independent administration? I did. Think of the extra fees involved with all of the motions they have to file? It's a probate lawyer's paradise. Don't let that happen to you.

7

How to Avoid Probate: It's ALL about the Character of the Asset

If you take nothing else from this book, take this:

Probate is not triggered by your death. It's triggered by what you leave behind—and how you leave it.

It all comes down to the **character of your assets.**

If you leave behind *probate assets*, you're going to probate. No matter what your Will says. No matter what your intentions were.

And the tragedy? Most people have no idea about this. They do what they think is responsible—they get a Will—thinking they've protected their family after their death.

But they haven't.

They've handed their family a stack of court paperwork and six months of legal bills.

Let me give it to you straight.

Probate doesn't just take time.
It takes money. A lot of it.

According to *SmartAsset,* probate eats up **3% to 10%** of the estate's value—and drags on anywhere from **6 to 20 months.**

Inheritance Advanced estimates that probate strips away **$2 billion every year** from families in this country. That's $2 billion that never makes it to the intended people.

So if your estate is worth $300,000, you're looking at a $9,000 to $30,000 loss. Just to get your own assets into the hands of your family.

And the worst part?

It's **completely avoidable.**

Every time someone dies with probate assets, they're handing a chunk of their estate straight to the court system. Probate assets are things like bank accounts, real estate, and investments held in your name only.

However, you can change the **character** of the asset and remove it from probate.

That's the goal I'm aiming for here. It's all about changing the character of your assets and keeping your money in the family, where it belongs.

I had a case not long ago—one of the few probates I've done in years. Husband and wife died nine days apart. Nine days. The kids didn't have access to the money. We had to probate the estate. Twice. Once for the husband and once more for the wife.

Two different judges. Two different clerks. Two different courts. Two different coordinators. Same family. Same paperwork. Same set of assets. It was identical both times, but we still had to go through probate the second time. That complicated things.

And you know what complicated means in my legal world?

Expensive.

All of it could've been avoided if the character of the bank accounts had been changed from probate assets to non-probate assets.

So let's talk a little more about what **probate** actually means.

When you die, the world needs to know who gets your stuff. A lot of people think that when they die, their spouse automatically gets their stuff.

And that's just not always the case, and it sure isn't automatic.

One way you can tell the world who gets your stuff is through a Will. You can say in your Will, "I want so-and-so to get my stuff." But if you go that route, you are most assuredly going to probate as we have already clearly pointed out. Because probate is the *only* way for a Will to have life.

Remember Frankenstein's monster and the lightning zap?

With the lightning zap, the monster is given life.

Probate is the lightning zap to a Will.

The Will has to be sent to the probate court, and then six months or so later, there's a hearing. The judge will dust off your Will, stick those "electrodes" in it, and *zing*—the Will will be given life. That's probate.

And, remember as I have already said, if that Will does not go to probate, then it's not worth the paper it's written on.

Thirty years ago, when I was a young lawyer and started doing probate work, I decided right away there must be a better way to handle estates. Probate was brutal. It was (and is) painstaking and time-consuming.

Worst of all, it was doing a disservice to the client, because the client didn't get access to the assets they needed to move forward. And they deserved to move forward. But they couldn't, not for months and months on end.

And the unbelievable truth is, all of that aggravation is avoidable.

When people call me and ask if I do Wills, I do say, "Yes, I do Wills," and then I also ask, "but would you be willing to entertain an idea where you don't ever have to use the Will? Where your loved ones can inherit your property the moment after you die?"

That sounds great, right?

Here's where that conversation starts.

The Will only has jurisdiction over what we call **probate assets.**

So, your assets are categorized into one of two different buckets. One bucket is for probate assets, and one bucket is for non-probate assets. Now, the best way to explain this decision is that any asset that you own in your own name is a probate asset—house, car, bank account, whatever. If it's in your name—Lance Sweets, David Goodhart, Mary Smith—then it's a probate asset.

Here's the big thing about this classification—the **probate court** and the **Will** have jurisdiction only over probate assets, but (here's the legal magic) **not over non-probate assets.**

Wouldn't it be fantastic if you could change a probate asset into a non-probate asset that your loved ones would inherit immediately, no muss, no fuss?

What if, while you're alive, you could choose the character of your assets? What if you could choose to move your assets from probate assets to non-probate assets?

Is there a mechanism where you can change the asset character of your house? Your bank accounts? Whatever else you've got?

What about your golf clubs? Your fine china? Your jewelry? All that personal property? It's still considered to be in your name. It's part of your estate. They are probate assets.

So unless you do something to change that, the **probate court has jurisdiction** over those things as well.

Essentially, if you die with assets in your own name, your heirs are going to probate.

I always tell clients, "It's all about the character of the asset." That's what matters.

At this point, I hope you see the "problem" with dealing with probate assets.

Now, are you ready for the solution?

We convert assets from probate assets to non-probate assets. Yes, it can be done!

Let's start with two documents that do big work to make this conversion happen.

8

How to Keep Your House and Bank Accounts Out of Probate Automatically

There are two powerful tools that make it possible to keep assets like your house and bank accounts out of probate: **Transfer on Death Deeds** and **Payable on Death features for bank accounts.**

They're simple, effective legal methods, and, if used correctly, they make probate completely unnecessary for your most valuable assets.

That's why it is important to review your estate on an asset-by-asset basis. Is there a vacation home? An interest in an LLC? Are there rental properties? Multiple bank accounts?

Once you have done this review, you can work with an attorney experienced in this field to determine what action to take for each asset to turn it from a probate asset to a non-probate asset.

Let's look at the simplest example: a client who has just a house and a bank account or two.

Perfect.

In two steps this client can protect the estate assets: 1) a Transfer on Death Deed (TOD) for the home and 2) a Payable on Death feature (POD) for the bank accounts.

There's just no reason to go to probate to make sure the house and the bank accounts get to your loved ones.

If we handle the paperwork now by utilizing TOD deeds and POD accounts, we save your family months of grief, thousands in legal fees, and a whole lot of stress. Let's take a look at them in a little more detail.

9

Beneficiary Designations

Any asset that has a beneficiary designation avoids probate.

That's the rule.

So what does it take to have a beneficiary designation?

Transfer on Death Deed

Since 2015, we've had this special kind of deed in Texas called a Transfer on Death Deed, also referred to as a TOD. It's a deed the client signs now and then files as required in the public records. But it doesn't do anything right now. It floats in the title cloud as long as the client is alive, and ownership stays in the client's name until they die.

And when they die? The person (or persons) listed as the beneficiary in the Transfer on Death Deed inherits whatever the deed is tied to—a house, for instance—automatically. No probate. Done deal.

Now, let's say you're living in Texas and have a TOD on your home, but it's hot, and you decide that you want to move someplace cooler. Maybe Alaska. To do that, you need to sell your house. No problem. The Transfer on Death Deed can be undone by you during your lifetime with the stroke of a pen. You can cancel it anytime for any reason and do whatever you want with the property, including sell it. But if you don't cancel it—and you die owning that home—then it's going to the beneficiaries, probate-free.

That make sense?

What you have done with this TOD deed is change the *character* of your house from a probate asset to a non-probate asset. You control it during your lifetime, and you name who receives the property after your death. You can even divide the ownership in equal portions. Or 70/30. Or 90/10. Whatever you want and to whomever you want, so, yes, you can leave it to all of your children. Doesn't matter if you've got one child or many children, it can be done.

The probate court now has no jurisdiction over the property. Your Will? Doesn't matter. The TOD rules.

This is a clean, simple way to take care of the home or other real estate property.

Occasionally people have very specific ideas about how they want to divide up their personal property.

In these cases, I might offer other solutions besides a Transfer on Death Deed. But for most clients, this strategy works beautifully.

Now what about the bank accounts?

Similar concept.

Payable on Death

This document, often called a POD, turns a bank account in your name into a non-probate asset by naming who it is payable to upon your death. Probate court and your Will? No jurisdiction!

Taking care of this is easy to do. You make an appointment with your banker and you explain that you want to put a Payable on Death feature on each of your accounts. The banker will know exactly what you mean.

You tell the bank specifically who is to receive the money in this account upon your death. Maybe it's your children. Or your spouse. Maybe someone else. But the takeaway is making the decision now who will inherit your bank accounts without your loved ones having to go to probate to get access to them.

Your Assets

It is advisable to go through your estate asset by asset. These TOD and POD measures are specific for a given asset, but work for all of your assets, even if you have multiple properties or multiple bank accounts.

It is important, then, to start converting each of your assets into "non-probate assets" by utilizing one or more Transfer on Death Deeds or putting in place Payable on Death features on your bank accounts.

So, if the only assets in your estate are a house and some bank accounts, and you've got a Transfer on Death Deed for the house and a Payable on Death feature on file for each bank account, you are set for your most valuable assets.

At your death, you have no probate assets because utilizing those devices changed the character of those assets into non-probate assets. So, there's nothing to probate. And, if you do have a Will? Well, it's moot.

That's the game we're playing here.

Of course, there are the contents of the house to be considered. Most of that usually travels with the house. The furniture, the stuff inside, the family heirlooms. That's a conversation you can have with your family. You may wish to jot down distribution preferences or special requests on a separate document, but it's not required.

Now, let me tell you a story to illustrate how powerful utilizing these two beneficiary measures can be.

Let's say my wife passes away, and I go do some estate planning. I execute a Transfer on Death Deed leaving my house to my kids. I go to the bank, set up Payable on Death designations and make my kids the beneficiaries of my bank accounts.

And then . . . I get married again.

My new wife convinces me to redo my Will. So I do. I leave *all* my worldly possessions to my new wife. That's what the Will says—everything to my surviving wife.

Then I die.

My wife assumes she's got it all.

But pretty soon, her lawyer is going to find out that I died owning no probate assets. The house? Already passed to my kids via TOD. The bank accounts? Also set to bypass the Will with PODs.

She gets nothing. My kids get everything.

And that's 100 percent legal.

So let's pause for a moment to make a really important point. People don't always understand this. They say, "But wait, the Will says X!" That may be true, but the Transfer on Death Deed says Y. And, the POD is clear too.

They don't get why the Will doesn't somehow override everything. But remember, the Will only has jurisdiction over probate assets, and once a TOD or a POD is implemented, the asset it covers becomes a non-probate asset.

This is the bottom line on that: **The Transfer on Death Deed and/or the Payable on Death feature trumps the Will.** Either or both will take precedence. The probate court and your Will have no jurisdiction anymore over those assets.

10

More Ways to Make Sure the House, the Bank Account, Other Property Go to the Right Person without Probate

There's another tool that can make sure the house, property holdings, and bank accounts go to the intended party directly upon your death. It's called **Joint Tenancy with Rights of Survivorship**—or **JTWROS** for short. By adding those magic words at the signing of a deed or bank form, your property bypasses probate and automatically goes to the other party on the deed or bank form. It's as simple as that. But you need to know about that option to make it happen.

Here's how it plays out in real life.

A woman came into my office once after her father passed away. She had the keys to the house, she'd been paying the mortgage, and she'd even lived there with him the last few years to help out.

When he died, she thought the house was hers. "We both lived there," she said. "I helped pay for it. Dad always told me it would be mine."

But when we pulled the deed, guess what it showed?

Just his name.

No joint tenancy. No survivorship language. No Transfer on Death Deed. Nothing.

So now we had a problem. That house, the one she thought was hers, was a **probate asset.**

We had to open a probate estate. File a petition. Wait for a court date. Track down other heirs. Pay court costs. All for a house she thought she already owned.

If he had just titled the property as **joint tenants with rights of survivorship,** it would've been hers the moment he passed. No court. No hassle.

That's what joint tenancy does.

It tells the world, "When I go, it goes to them." Automatically.

Here's another example. This one involves business property and non-family owners.

Let's say two people buy a shopping center together, but the title lists the two new owners as follows: **Lance Sweet and Jack Spratly, as joint tenants with rights of survivorship,** using the magic language.

If one of them dies, the surviving owner takes over his partner's portion of the ownership automatically, directly, and immediately. There is no dealing with the family or heirs of the deceased person whatsoever. The power of the Joint Tenancy with Right of Survivorship controls the ownership.

Nolo, a trusted legal publisher since 1971, calls joint tenancy "the most popular probate-avoidance device around." It's simple, effective—and **costs nothing to set up.**

That's not fluff. It can have a real impact on how things end up down the road. One simple step at signing a deed or bank form, and your property bypasses probate automatically.

Whether it's a home, property, or a bank account, properly setting up a JTWROS instantly transfers the deceased's share to the surviving co-owner—no court, no delays, no legal fees.

This concept is somewhat unique to Texas. It's not applicable across all 50 states. But, here in Texas, Joint Tenancy with Right of Survivorship is a real option when taking title with someone else.

You can even do it with your spouse.

A lot of times, it shows up in a bank account. You can open a bank account, and while you're setting it up, you tell the banker:

> *"Oh, by the way, I want this to be JTWROS—Joint Tenancy with Rights of Survivorship."*

And they'll know exactly what you mean.

In fact, sometimes, when you get your bank statement in the mail, it'll actually reflect the status right on the statement:

Mr. and Mrs. Smith – JTWROS

That's the clue.

It's telling the world that you own that asset jointly, with survivorship rights. And that means when Mr. Smith dies, Mrs. Smith automatically inherits his one-half interest in that account, and if Mrs. Smith dies first, Mr. Smith inherits her one-half interest in that account.

11

A Trust

I want to give you one more key strategy for avoiding probate in your estate planning: the **inter vivos trust.** Inter vivos is Latin for "during your lifetime." An inter vivos trust is something you create while you're alive—not in the body of your Will. A trust, of course, is separate from, and, as you will see below, replaces your Will.

Step one is to create the trust.

Step two is to fund it.

You have to actually transfer the title of your assets into the name of the trust. A trust with no assets is like no trust at all. Assets transferred to the trust are protected from probate, because assets owned by a trust are considered non-probate assets.

This just happened recently. A client called me and said he had created a trust 15 years ago but never retitled a single asset to it. Nothing.

My response was, "Thank God you called me before you died." And I was serious.

We were able to retitle his assets into the trust and, yes, avoid probate altogether as was intended at the inception of the trust. But if the client hadn't come to me? If the client had passed away? The empty trust would have done nothing for the heirs. All the assets would have gone through probate.

Utilizing a trust is one of my favorite probate-avoidance strategies. While not everyone needs a trust, I tend to lean toward using them when the client has multiple assets, like multiple properties, or one or more businesses. Otherwise, I will default to using a combination of TODs, PODs, and JTWROS strategies.

12

Why Don't More Estate Planners Talk about Avoiding Probate?

If avoiding probate is so simple—and it is—then why doesn't every estate planner walk you through these steps?

Here's the truth most folks don't want to say out loud:

There's a lot of money in probate.

A lot.

I'm talking about court fees, attorney fees, executor fees, accounting fees. Every delay, every filing, every contested document—it all adds up. And the longer it takes? The more everyone gets paid.

According to industry estimates, **over $2 billion is drained from American families every single year** just by going through probate. That's not lost due to theft. That's not mismanagement. That's the cost of doing it the "normal" way.

So what happens?

Well, the average estate planning attorney does just enough to make you feel like you've handled things. They give you a Will. They get it signed. Maybe they toss in a medical power of attorney. You leave the office thinking you've protected your family.

But what did you really do?

You just paid for the front end of the job—and left the back end wide open.

Dad had all of his affairs "taken care of." He told the family that if anything ever happened, they just needed to call the number on the emergency card in his estate planning binder. He said everything was in place.

So that's what they did. First call after the funeral—straight to the law firm on the card.

But the attorney who drafted the Will? He had retired. Then passed away a few years later. The firm transferred the son to one of their "probate specialists"—someone who had no idea who his dad even was.

Didn't stop the specialist from asking for **several thousand dollars up front** just to get started.

And get this—he wanted to *charge* the son just to sit down and walk through the same documents his own firm had prepared.

The son asked, "Can we just pay you from Dad's account?" The lawyer told him he would have to cover it out of pocket, because he won't be able to touch his dad's money until everything was filed and approved by the court. And that could take six to eight months, maybe longer.

The worst part?

Dad wasn't good with paperwork. He hated computers. There was no master list. No account summary. No passwords. They had no idea where the money even was—just a Will and a binder, and now a growing legal bill that wasn't planned for.

And that's the game they play.

You get sold the "peace of mind" up front, but there's probate to cash in on later.

So, when you die, your family has to come back and pay for the rest. That's the business model. It's not illegal. It's not even deceptive—because technically, they did what you asked. You said you needed a Will. And that's what they gave you.

But then you didn't know to ask the best question, **"How do I avoid probate altogether?"**

And they didn't offer it up. Why didn't they?

Because many probate lawyers who do estate planning aren't looking out for **YOUR** best interests. They **KNOW** that by only providing a Will, your heirs are going straight to probate, but if they tell you that **you really need more than a Will,** then they won't get the probate work on the back end. At a minimum, I think it's reprehensible. At most, I think it's malpractice.

And unless you talk to someone who's willing to pull back the curtain—someone who says, "You don't actually need to go through probate at all"—you would never know there was an option in the first place.

This is why I wrote this book.

Because the system isn't broken, It's doing exactly what it was designed to do. But that means you're the one who has to ask for more than a Will. You've got to be the one to ask the best question—"How do I avoid probate?"

And that brings up another fun little side note about all those legal forms you can get off the internet.

I'm not here to besmirch anybody, but you probably know some of the names.

And I'd bet you—this would be a fun little exercise for readers—I'd bet you those sample Wills probably don't include the magic language to avoid dependent administration in administering a Texas Will. I bet there are no measures incorporated to avoid probate altogether.

However, one thing I can tell you for sure: on my forms website—TexasLegalForms.com—my sample Will does include the magic language you need to keep your family out of dependent administration, not to mention other forms necessary for changing the character of your assets to avoid probate. Pay attention to these simple things and you will protect your assets for your intended heirs.

The Worst Gift You Can Leave Behind Is Probate.

Maintenance

When I prepare a Will, a Trust, or any kind of estate planning tool, I always ask my clients:

> *"Has there been a big-ticket event? That's your red caution flag. That's your moment to pause and review your estate plan."*

It is so important to keep your plan updated with the flow of events that naturally occur in life. Always use the POD where you are allowed to do so when you set up new financial accounts. Create TODs for your significant assets and have your spouse do the same. Or use a JTWROS or an inter vivos trust.

Review your asset protections periodically to make sure nothing is missing and everything is up to date. Has a beneficiary passed away? Was a new member born into the family? Has some marital status changed? Update as needed! **And make certain everything has been filed and recorded as necessary.**

But too often most people don't do these things. If they sign a Will, they tend to let it sit and forget about it. And their loved ones are the ones stuck with the headaches and heartaches and cleaning up the mess later.

That's why I say this again and again: you need quality, expert advice, **especially from someone who isn't pushing a Will all by itself.** And you need to review your plan periodically, especially when a big event has occurred in your life.

Don't depend on guesswork or a cheap online form or your neighbor's cousin who once filed a deed. Take the appropriate measures to protect your family, no matter the size of your estate. They will thank you later even though you are gone.

13

Summary of Key Points

Talking points:

Best question: How to avoid probate

Important request: Independent administration

Establish PODs for bank accounts

Create TODs for major assets

Consider other measures like JTWROS and inter vivos trust

Maintain and update as needed

Protect your family from the headaches of probate

About the author . . .

David is a native of Overland Park, Kansas, although he has lived in Texas most of his life. He has been practicing law since 1994 and has extensive real estate and estate-planning experience. David stopped taking on probate clients years ago, devoting his practice instead to keeping clients out of probate. An expert troubleshooter by nature, David takes pleasure in solving the thorniest of problems.

For more information about David, please visit:
DavidGoodhartPLLC.com

For helpful resources, please visit:
TexasLegalForms.com

Made in the USA
Monee, IL
04 November 2026

67767539R00036